I SPY

GOLD CHALLENGER!

A BOOK OF
PICTURE
RIDDLES

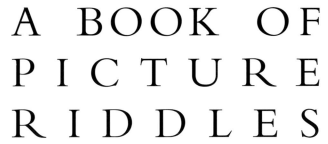

Photographs by Walter Wick

Riddles by Jean Marzollo

Cartwheel
·B·O·O·K·S·®

SCHOLASTIC INC.
New York Toronto London Auckland Sydney
Mexico City New Delhi Hong Kong Buenos Aires

For my mother

—————
W.W.

For Clorae Evereteze Prince Diaz
—————
J.M.

Book design by Carol Devine Carson

Go to www.scholastic.com for Web site information
on Scholastic authors and illustrators.

"Toy Chest" and "Cubbies" from I Spy © 1992 by Walter Wick; "Winter Sports" from I Spy Christmas
© 1992 by Walter Wick; "Sand Castle" and "Blast Off!" from I Spy Fantasy © 1994 by Walter Wick; "The
Birthday Hunt" and "The Ghost in the Attic" from I Spy Mystery © 1993 by Walter Wick; "Mapping,"
"Patterns & Paints," and "Levers, Ramps, & Pulleys" from I Spy School Days © 1995 by Walter Wick;
"Puppet Theater" from I Spy Fun House © 1993 by Walter Wick; "A Blazing Fire" from I Spy Spooky
Night © 1996 by Walter Wick. All published by Scholastic Inc.

Library of Congress Cataloging-in-Publication Data

Wick, Walter.
I spy gold challenger!: a book of picture riddles / photographs by Walter Wick; riddles
by Jean Marzollo.
p.   cm. — (I spy books)
Summary: Rhyming text leads the reader to find objects hidden in the photographs.
ISBN 0-590-04296-3
1. Picture puzzles—Juvenile literature.   2. Riddles
[1. Picture puzzles.]   I. Marzollo, Jean.   II. Title.   III. Series
GV1507.P47W5295   1998
793.735—dc21   98-13982
                                                                CIP
                                                                AC

0-590-04296-3 (pob)

12 11 10 9 8 7 6 5 4 3 2 1   5 6 7 8 9/0
Printed in Malaysia   46

Reinforced Library Edition
ISBN: 0-439-68426-9
This edition, March 2005

TABLE OF CONTENTS

Picture riddles fill this book;
Turn the pages! Take a look!

Use your mind, use your eye;
Read the riddles—play I SPY!

I spy a turtle, four ladders, and SAND,

Three baseball gloves, and a picture of land;

Four birdies of blue, nine bowling pins,
A balloon, a mask, and two swim fins.

I spy a heart, a starfish, a frog,
A towel, a trowel, a taxi, a dog;

Seven horses, a barrel, a duck that is teeny,
Two real feathers, and a surfer's bikini.

I spy a lamb, a candle, a van,

An old shoelace, and a potbellied man;

A baby bottle, a fancy shoe,
Two paper houses, and two giraffes, too.

I spy a spool, seven arrows, a veil,

A stop light, a meter, a small sack of mail;

An alligator car, a standing clothespin,
Fifty-six people, plus a happy grin.

I spy three musical instruments to play,
Two matches, a dog, a trunk, and a tray;

A triangle button, a small metal nail,
The shadow of a bat, and a lion's tail.

I spy a screw, a skateboard, a spring,
A turkey, a bottle, an elastic string;

REINDEER, RAILROAD, three smokestacks, a clock,
An ear with eyes, and a little blue sock.

I spy a ruler, a fan, two D's,

A puzzle piece, a bike, two V's;

Three ants, a giraffe, a green reptile,
A shoelace, a saw, and a bearded smile.

I spy a dustpan, a shutter, a cork,

Antlers, a drill bit, a boy, and a fork;

A feather, a wrench, two telephone poles,
A sewing machine, and a brick with holes.

I spy a hydrant, a platter, a 3,
A chain, a car, a kettle for tea;

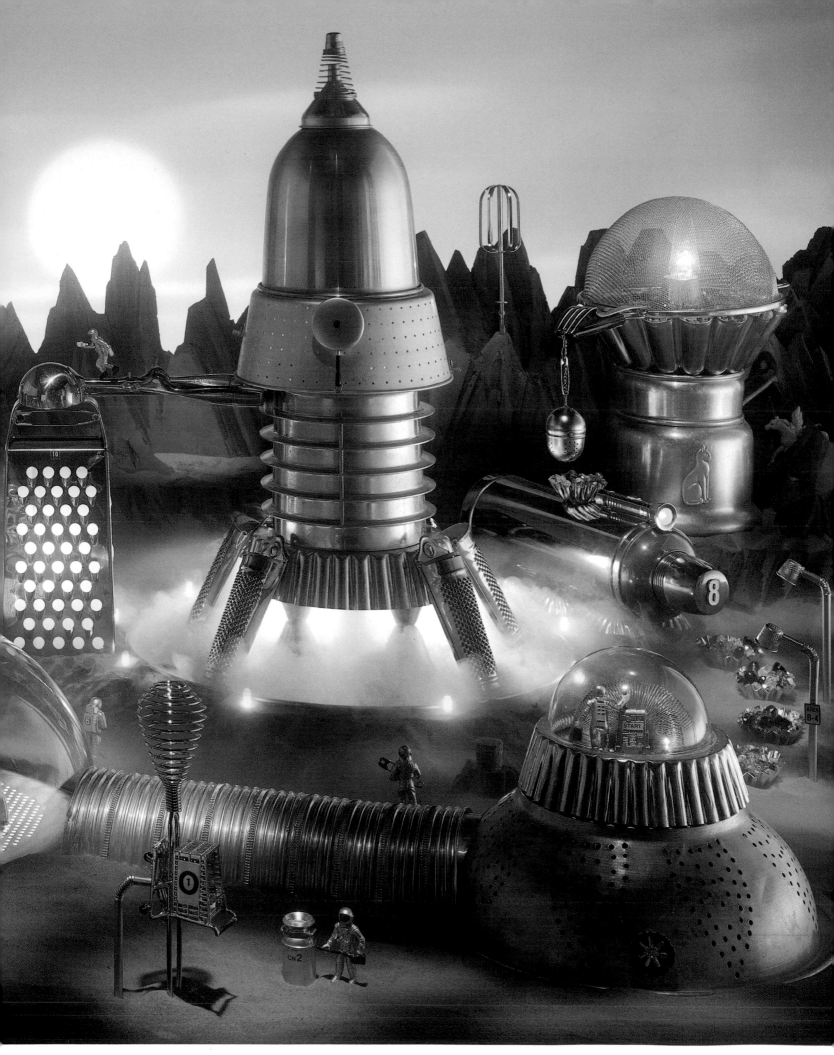

A bottle cap, a thimble spring,
Three silver straws, and a feathery wing.

I spy a sailboat, a ruler, a D,

A polka-dot sock, four cats, and TEA;

Five paper clips, and a panda bear,
And two white birds that aren't really there.

I spy an acorn, an upside-down STAR,
Goggles, suspenders, a red race car;

Two white beards, a moon, a lock,
Six bears, seven hats, and a snowy sock.

I spy two pencils, and a porcupine,

Two cups, a nut, and a double nine;

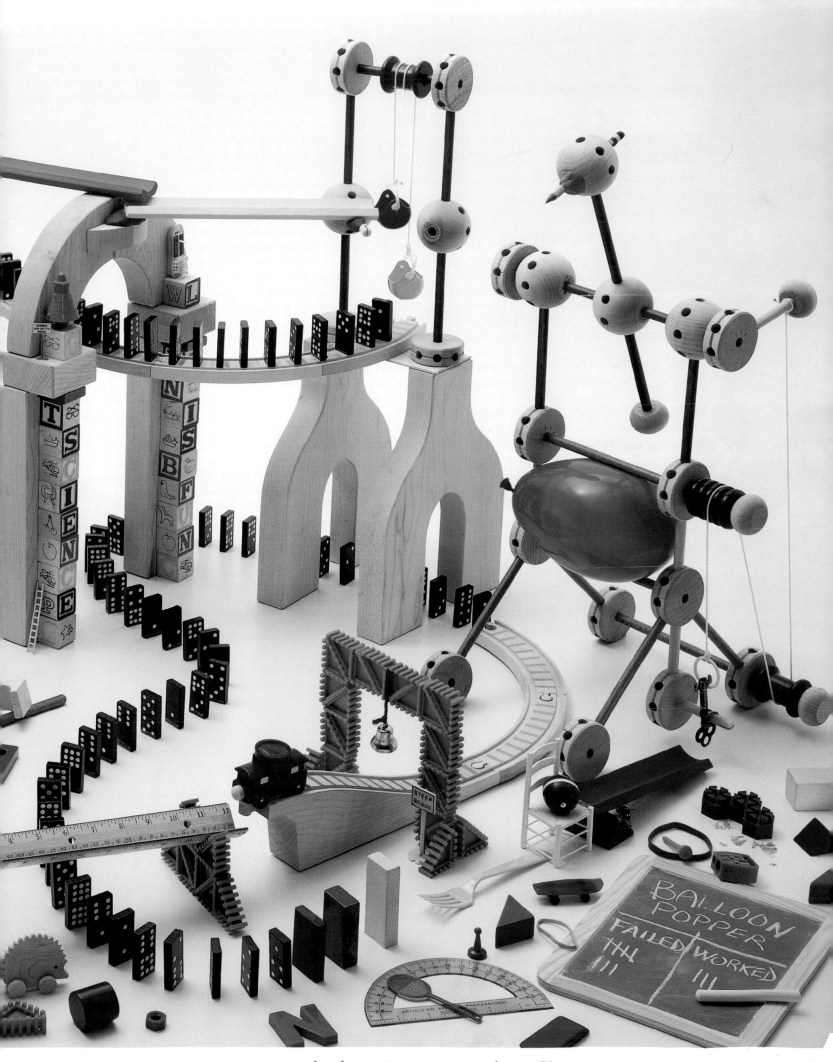

Two straws, wood shavings on the floor,
And something that's also on page 24.

EXTRA CREDIT RIDDLES

Find the Pictures That Go With These Riddles:

I spy a dog, a tight yellow knot,

A yellow boot, and something that's hot.

I spy a marble that's red and white,

Two googly eyes, a gear, and a knight.

I spy a swan, a red-and-yellow flower,

A spool, a drum, and a little white tower.

I spy two arrows, a domino, a chain,

Two hot bones, and a horse's mane.

I spy a seashell, toe prints, a tree,

A guy with no shirt, and a ship at sea.

I spy a peanut, a small rolling pin,

Two horses, a broom, and a dorsal fin.

I spy a broom, a fork, a TV,

A vertical boat, and a little golf tee.

I spy a price code, a graph paper plan,

A hungry blue ape, and a briefcase man.

I spy a nutcracker, a magnet man,

Three T's, a B, and a frying pan.

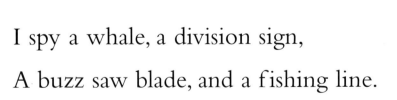

I spy two dinosaurs, a machine that can mix,

A clown that pours, and a double six.

I spy a whale, a division sign,

A buzz saw blade, and a fishing line.

I spy a stroller, clock hands, and GO,

MILK'S THE ONE, a hydrant, and SLOW.

Write Your Own Picture Riddles

There are many more hidden objects and many more possibilities for riddles in this book. Write some rhyming picture riddles yourself, and try them out with friends.

About the Creators of *I Spy*

Jean Marzollo has written many award-winning children's books including the I Spy books, *Ten Cats Have Hats, Pretend You're a Cat, Close Your Eyes, Home Sweet Home*, and *Sun Song*. She is the author of acclaimed nonfiction for children including *I Am Water, In 1492*, and *Happy Birthday, Martin Luther King*, and popular books for beginning readers including *Football Friends, Hockey Hero*, and *Soccer Cousins*. For nineteen years, Jean Marzollo and Carol Carson produced Scholastic's kindergarten magazine, *Let's Find Out*. Ms. Marzollo holds a master's degree from the Harvard Graduate School of Education. She lives with her husband, Claudio, in Cold Spring, New York.

Walter Wick is the photographer of the I Spy books including *I Spy: A Book of Picture Riddles, I Spy Christmas, I Spy Fun House*, and *I Spy Spooky Night*. He is both author and photographer of *A Drop of Water: A Book of Science and Wonder*, an ALA Notable Book and winner of the Boston Globe/Horn Book Award for nonfiction, and *Walter Wick's Optical Tricks*. Prior to creating children's books, Mr. Wick invented photographic games for *Games* magazine and photographed more than 300 covers for books and magazines, including *Newsweek, Discover, Psychology Today*, and Scholastic's *Let's Find Out* and *Super Science*. Mr. Wick is a graduate of Paier College of Art. He lives with his wife, Linda, in New York and Connecticut.

Carol Devine Carson, the book designer for the I Spy series, is art director for a major publishing house in New York City.

A Letter From the Creators of *I Spy Gold Challenger!*

Dear Readers,

Two ideas came together to inspire *I Spy Gold Challenger!* First, we began to notice that among all the I Spy photographs, we have our favorites. Of course, we love them all, but there are twelve pictures that we like best. Executive editor Grace Maccarone noticed that our choices are her favorites, too. "Let's put them together in one book," we said. "We can call it *I Spy Golden Greats.*"

The second idea came from kids. Kids everywhere have been telling us that they love solving the super-hard riddles in *I Spy Super Challenger!* precisely because they are so challenging. These kids asked for another *Challenger!* Could we do both? "Yes," said Bernette Ford, editorial director of Cartwheel Books, "and you can call it *I Spy Gold Challenger!*"

For those of you who love to find every single thing in every single riddle, including the Extra Credit riddles, this book is for you. Here are some tips for success: (1) Make sure you have a good light on the page. (2) Work together. Two or three minds may be better than one! (3) If you don't know what a word means, ask someone. That's how you learn.

We'd like to thank the many children and their teachers who tested these riddles for us: Adam, Catherine, Chloe, Emily, Heather, Holland, James, Jonathan, Katie, Kaylee, Lindsey, Max, Rozele, Wyatt, Zach, and Mrs. Donna Norkeliunas; Lana, Julia, Emily, Diana, Chelsea, Ari, Daniella, Lucas, Ryan, Darryl, Max, John, Marty, Erica, Jeff, Anna, Dylan, Will, Johanna, Matt A., Matt H., Joel, Raymond, Ed, James, Kim, Maike, and Ms. Katie Brennan; Molly, Matt, Clea, and Zak. We'd also like to thank David Marzollo once again for his outstanding creative input.

Happy Hunting!

Jean Marzollo and Walter Wick

Other I Spy books:

I SPY: A BOOK OF PICTURE RIDDLES

New York Public Library: One Hundred Titles — For Reading and Sharing;
California Children's Media Award, Honorable Mention

I SPY CHRISTMAS: A BOOK OF PICTURE RIDDLES

Parents Magazine, Best Books List

I SPY FUN HOUSE: A BOOK OF PICTURE RIDDLES

Publishers Weekly's Best Books of 1993; American Bookseller Pick of the Lists

I SPY MYSTERY: A BOOK OF PICTURE RIDDLES

Publishers Weekly's Best Books of 1993; American Bookseller Pick of the Lists;
National Parenting Publications Award, Honorable Mention

I SPY FANTASY: A BOOK OF PICTURE RIDDLES

Book-Of-The-Month Club Main Selection

I SPY SCHOOL DAYS: A BOOK OF PICTURE RIDDLES

American Bookseller Pick of the Lists;
New York Public Library: One Hundred Titles — For Reading and Sharing

I SPY SPOOKY NIGHT: A BOOK OF PICTURE RIDDLES

Book-Of-The-Month Club Main Selection

I SPY SUPER CHALLENGER!: A BOOK OF PICTURE RIDDLES

And for the youngest child:

I SPY LITTLE BOOK

I SPY LITTLE ANIMALS

I SPY LITTLE WHEELS

Also available:

I SPY CD-ROM

Oppenheim Toy Portfolio Platinum Award; Home PC Reviewers' Choice Award;
Thunderbeam Best Game for Kids; Parents' Choice Seal of Approval
Bologna New Media Prize for Logic